The Marquis de Lafayette and Other International Champions of the American Revolution

Beth Henrickson

NEW YORK

Published in 2016 by The Rosen Publishing Group, Inc.
29 East 21st Street, New York, NY 10010

Copyright © 2016 by The Rosen Publishing Group, Inc.

Photo Credits: Cover Library of Congress Prints and Photographs Division; p. 4 Library of Congress Newspaper
and Periodicals Reading Room; p. 5 Time Life Pictures/Getty Images; pp. 6, 10, 14, 16, Hulton Fine Art Collection/
Getty Images; p. 7 Universal Images Group/Superstock; pp. 9, 17 Buyenlarge/Archive Photos/Getty Images; p. 11
Universal History Archive/UIG/Getty Images; p. 13 SuperStock; p. 15 Château de Versailles, France/Bridgeman
Images; p. 18 Kean Collection/Archive Photos/Getty Images; p. 19 PhotoQuest/Archive Photos/Getty images; p.
20 Fotosearch/Archive Photos/Getty Images; p. 21 Fototeca Storica Nazionale/Hulton Archive/Getty images

Library of Congress Cataloging-in-Publication Data

Henrickson, Beth.
 The Marquis de Lafayette and other international champions of the American Revolution / Beth Henrickson. --
First edition.
     pages cm. -- (Spotlight on American history)
 Includes bibliographical references and index.
 ISBN 978-1-4994-1747-0 (library bound) -- ISBN 978-1-4994-1745-6 (pbk.) -- ISBN 978-1-4994-1744-9
(6-pack)
1. United States--History--Revolution, 1775-1783--Participation, Foreign--Juvenile literature. 2. United States--
History--Revolution, 1775-1783--Biography--Juvenile literature. 3. Revolutionaries--United States--Biography--
Juvenile literature. 4. Soldiers--United States--Biography--Juvenile literature. I. Title.
 E269.F67H46 2016
 973.3'2--dc23
                                    2015014365

Manufactured in the United States of America

CPSIA Compliance Information: Batch #WS15PK: For Further Information contact Rosen Publishing, New York, New York at 1-800-237-9932

CONTENTS

THE AMERICAN FIGHT FOR INDEPENDENCE.....4

THE MARQUIS DE LAFAYETTE: FOR THE LOVE OF LIBERTY..........6

FRENCH KING LOUIS XVI SUPPORTS THE AMERICANS 10

LAFAYETTE AND LOUIS XVI..........12

COMTE DE ROCHAMBEAU AND 6,000 FRENCH SOLDIERS 14

ADMIRAL DE GRASSE AND THE FRENCH FLEET..........16

BARON DE KALB: MAJOR GENERAL OF THE CONTINENTAL ARMY 18

BARON VON STEUBEN: INSPECTOR GENERAL ..20

COUNT CASIMIR PULASKI AND THE AMERICAN CAVALRY..........22

GLOSSARY..........23

INDEX..........24

PRIMARY SOURCE LIST 24

WEBSITES..........24

THE AMERICAN FIGHT FOR INDEPENDENCE

From 1775 to 1783, the American colonies fought for **independence** from Britain. This war was called the American Revolution. In 1775, Britain was one of the richest and most powerful countries in the world. It had many soldiers and a powerful navy. The American colonists had little money, few soldiers, and no navy. In addition, the Americans had to fight in their own land,

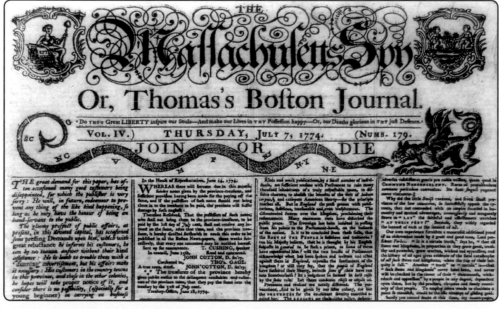

The front page of the Massachusetts Spy can be seen here. The Spy was established in Boston in 1770 by Isaiah Thomas. The newspaper's rattlesnake was a symbol of the 13 colonies.

This drawing depicts the Battle of Bunker Hill. The battle was fought on June 17, 1775. The determination of the colonial militiamen can be seen as they confront the British troops.

where their homes and families were in danger. Often, they even had to fight against their own neighbors who did not want independence from Britain. These people were known as loyalists.

From the beginning of the revolution, the odds were against the American colonists. They welcomed any help they could get from other countries or from individual **volunteers** who were willing to fight for the cause of freedom.

THE MARQUIS DE LAFAYETTE: FOR THE LOVE OF LIBERTY

The Marquis de Lafayette was a volunteer who helped the American colonists fight for freedom. He was only 19 years old when he arrived in America. Lafayette was born in France on September 6, 1757. He was a rich, young **nobleman** from a well-known military family. His father had died fighting the British

This portrait of Gilbert Motier, the Marquis de Lafayette, was painted in 1834. It shows Lafayette as a lieutenant general during the American Revolutionary War.

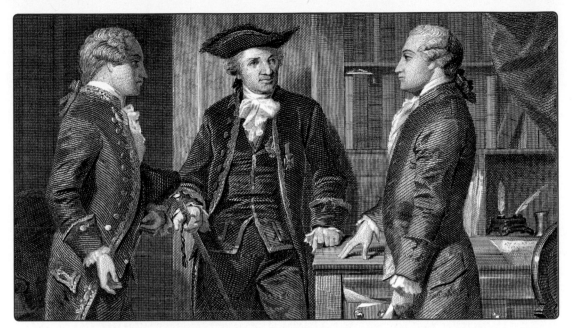

This engraving records the famous meeting between Lafayette and Silas Deane in Paris. Lafayette is being introduced to Deane by Baron de Kalb.

in the Seven Years' War when Lafayette was only three years old. When Lafayette was young, he dreamed of winning glory on the battlefield.

Young French noblemen were often educated to become officers to fight for France. Lafayette trained with the son of the king of France, Louis XVI. Lafayette became an officer, but later, with changes in the French army, he lost his position.

In December 1776, Lafayette was introduced to Silas Deane, the American delegate to France. Deane told Lafayette and Baron Johann de Kalb, a German professional soldier who fought for France, about the American War for

Independence. Deane told them that he was trying to get French support for the American cause. He also promised high rank to French officers willing to fight for the American colonists. He promised Lafayette the rank of major general. This was a very high rank for a man so young. Lafayette asked King Louis XVI for permission to fight in America. The king did not give permission.

In 1777, Lafayette secretly bought a ship called *La Victoire* (Victory) to sail to America against the king's wishes. If the king caught Lafayette, he would go to jail. Baron de Kalb and Lafayette moved the ship to Spain and set sail from there. It took them seven weeks to reach South Carolina. Lafayette used the time on the ship to practice his English.

Lafayette and Baron de Kalb then made an 800-mile (1,287 kilometer) trip to Philadelphia on land. When Lafayette met the American colonial leaders in Philadelphia, he told them that he would fight without pay. Lafayette became a major general, as Silas Deane had promised. Lafayette served under General George Washington.

Lafayette fought in the Battle of Brandywine on September 11, 1777. He showed great courage on the battlefield. He was wounded in the leg but continued

This 1777 engraving of the Battle of Brandywine shows all the drama of the fight.

fighting. The British defeated the Americans at the Battle of Brandywine, but Lafayette won the admiration of the Americans. General Washington especially came to value the young Frenchman.

On December 1, 1777, Lafayette was given his own regiment to lead. He bought his men their **equipment** and clothing with his own money. On June 28, 1778, Lafayette and his men fought bravely at the Battle of Monmouth, helping General Washington to fight to a draw against the British lieutenant general Sir Henry Clinton. Though the Americans did not win the battle, they showed how strong they had become.

FRENCH KING LOUIS XVI SUPPORTS THE AMERICANS

The Americans lost many battles early in the American Revolution. They soon realized that they would need help from other countries to win the war. In March 1776, Silas Deane and Benjamin Franklin asked France for help in America's fight against Britain.

This portrait of the French king Louis XVI by Joseph-Siffred Duplessis was painted in 1754. This work was designed to show the power and wealth of the French king.

This illustration shows British general Burgoyne's surrender to American soldiers after the Battle of Saratoga in 1777.

Britain was France's enemy. The French king, Louis XVI, saw a chance to weaken Britain. The French began to send money and guns secretly to the Americans. At first, Louis XVI did not want to support the colonists openly. He was not sure the colonists could win. However, after the American victory at Saratoga in 1777, Louis XVI decided to support the Americans openly.

LAFAYETTE AND LOUIS XVI

Lafayette returned to France after the Battle of Monmouth to help the American cause. The Americans gave him a letter to give to King Louis XVI. The letter said how brave and helpful Lafayette had been in fighting against the British.

When he arrived in France, Lafayette told Louis XVI that he thought the French should invade England. The French king would not do this. He did agree to send six ships and 6,000 men to help the Americans. He also sent Lafayette back to America as his personal representative.

Lafayette arrived in Boston in April 1780. On September 5, 1781, 24 French warships and 3,000 French soldiers joined Lafayette in Williamsburg, Virginia. These soldiers and ships were about to fight what was to be the last important battle of the American Revolution.

At the Battle of Yorktown, Major General Lafayette was given the great honor to lead the first 400 men into battle. On October 19, 1781, 8,000 Hessian and British troops were forced to surrender to General Washington.

The British made a last stand at Yorktown. They were, however, no match for the combined forces of the American and French armies.

The French navy helped in the battle by blocking any British escape by sea. The Marquis de Lafayette played an important role in helping the Americans win the war and gain their independence from Britain.

COMTE DE ROCHAMBEAU AND 6,000 FRENCH SOLDIERS

The Comte de Rochambeau was an experienced French general who had shown his abilities in two major European wars. He was chosen by Louis XVI to lead the French soldiers in America. On May 1, 1780, he sailed from Brest, France, with around 6,000 men.

The French force arrived at Newport, Rhode Island, in July 1780. They remained there through the winter,

This beautiful oil painting by Charles Lariviere of the Comte de Rochambeau shows the general as a hero.

This oil painting documents the Siege of Yorktown on October 17, 1781. The Comte de Rochambeau and George Washington are giving orders for the attack.

while George Washington and Rochambeau decided what to do next. Washington wanted to attack the British in New York City. Rochambeau thought the British were too strong in New York. He wanted to attack British general Cornwallis in the south. When news arrived that Cornwallis was heading to Yorktown, Virginia, Washington decided to attack.

ADMIRAL DE GRASSE AND THE FRENCH FLEET

Admiral François Joseph Paul de Grasse was an experienced officer in the French navy. In 1781, Rochambeau asked de Grasse to sail with 3,000 soldiers and 24 ships from the West Indies to Virginia.

With Rochambeau's support, Washington planned to attack the British troops at Yorktown. De Grasse's fleet drove off the British navy and blocked the harbor to prevent the British from helping Cornwallis.

This portrait of Admiral de Grasse was painted in 1788. This was the last year of the admiral's life.

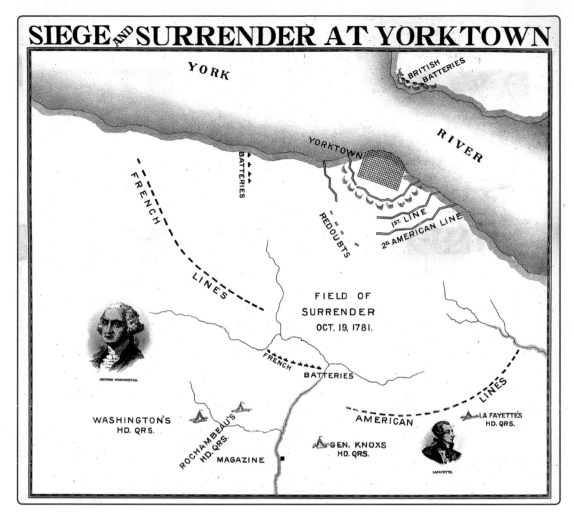

SIEGE & SURRENDER AT YORKTOWN

YORK

BRITISH BATTERIES

RIVER

YORKTOWN

FRENCH LINES

BATTERIES

REDOUBTS

1ST. LINE
2D. AMERICAN LINE

FIELD OF
SURRENDER
OCT. 19, 1781.

FRENCH
BATTERIES

GEORGE WASHINGTON.

WASHINGTON'S
HD. QRS.

ROCHAMBEAU'S
HD. QRS.

MAGAZINE

GEN. KNOXS
HD. QRS.

AMERICAN

LINES

LA FAYETTE'S
HD. QRS.

LAFAYETTE.

This map made in 1898 shows the battle lines during the siege and surrender at Yorktown.

On October 19, 1781, Cornwallis had to surrender because de Grasse was blocking his escape route by sea. This American victory led to the end of the war. In this battle, as in many others, the international military support was important to the success of America's fight for freedom.

BARON DE KALB: MAJOR GENERAL OF THE CONTINENTAL ARMY

Baron Johann de Kalb was a German-born French soldier who had fought in two major European wars. In 1776, he accepted a **commission** as a major general in the Continental army. He joined George Washington in 1777, at Valley Forge in Pennsylvania. He was sent south to be second in command under General Horatio Gates.

De Kalb was a decorated soldier in the French army before traveling to America to fight in the revolution. This engraving of de Kalb was made in 1770.

This dramatic engraving of 1780 documents a scene from the Battle of Camden. In this battle, Baron Johann de Kalb lost his life.

On August 16, 1780, Gates decided to attack Camden, South Carolina, where Lord Charles Cornwallis had a strong British force. Many of the American soldiers were **inexperienced**, and the British quickly defeated them. Even though the battle was lost, de Kalb did not give up. He and his men held their ground. Finally de Kalb fell, having suffered 11 wounds. He died on August 19, 1780.

BARON VON STEUBEN: INSPECTOR GENERAL

In February 1778, Baron Friedrich von Steuben arrived at the Continental army's camp at Valley Forge. He was introduced to George Washington as a **Prussian** lieutenant general. He volunteered to **train** the American soldiers.

Baron von Steuben was a confident and experienced officer. Charles Willson Peale painted this portrait in 1780.

Washington at Valley Forge is one of the most popular images of the American Revolution. This postcard was created in 1921. It shows Washington, with Lafayette and von Steuben, speaking to a sentry.

The American soldiers at Valley Forge were **undisciplined**. They also did not have proper equipment, but von Steuben quickly taught them how to fight like professional soldiers. He taught them the importance of cleanliness in the camp and how to fire a gun properly.

George Washington was impressed by von Steuben's training abilities. He made von Steuben the inspector general of the army. Baron von Steuben wrote the first **manual** for the army. It was known as the Blue Book.

COUNT CASIMIR PULASKI AND THE AMERICAN CAVALRY

Soldiers from many countries came to help the Americans. They did this because they believed in the American cause. Count Casimir Pulaski was a Polish soldier who had fought for Poland's independence from Russia. In 1776, Benjamin Franklin told him of the war in America, and Pulaski decided that he wanted to help the Americans. He helped to train the American **cavalry** and was placed in charge of it in 1777.

In 1778, he organized a cavalry, known as Pulaski's **Legion**. The legion was made up mostly of foreign volunteers. In 1779, his legion was sent to help recapture Savannah, Georgia, from the British. Pulaski was wounded during the battle. He died on October 11, 1779. Today he is known as the Father of the American Cavalry.

GLOSSARY

cavalry (KA-vul-ree) The part of an army that rides horses.

commission (kuh-MIH-shun) A document that gives a certain military rank or authority.

equipment (uh-KWIP-mint) All the supplies needed to do an activity.

independence (in-dih-PEN-dents) Freedom from the control, support, or help of others.

inexperienced (in-ek-SPEER-ee-unst) To be new at something.

legion (LEE-juhn) A unit in an army.

manual (MAN-yuh-wul) A guide or book that provides instructions for some activity.

nobleman (NOH-bul-man) A member of royalty or other high-ranking person in a kingdom.

Prussian (PRUH-shun) Native of Prussia, a former state in Germany.

train (TRAYN) To learn something through practice.

undisciplined (un-DIH-sih-plind) Without training or not used to following rules.

volunteers (vah-luhn-TEERZ) People who give their time without pay.

INDEX

B

Brandywine, Battle of, 8–9

Britain, 4–5, 10–11, 12, 13, 15, 16, 19, 22

C

colonies, 4, 11

Continental army, 18, 20

Cornwallis, Charles, 15, 16, 17, 19

D

Deane, Silas, 7–8, 10

de Grasse, François Paul, 16–17

de Kalb, Baron Johann, 7, 8, 18, 19

F

France, 6–7, 10–11, 12, 13, 14, 16, 18

Franklin, Benjamin, 10, 22

G

Gates, Horatio, 18, 19

L

Lafayette, Marquis de, 6–9, 12, 13

Louis XVI, 7, 8, 11, 12, 14

M

Monmouth, Battle of, 9, 12

P

Pulaski, Casimir, 22

R

Rochambeau, Comte de, 14–15, 16

V

Valley Forge, 18, 20–21

von Steuben, Baron Friedrich, 20–21

W

Washington, George, 8, 9, 12, 15, 16, 18, 20, 21

Y

Yorktown, Battle of, 12, 15, 16

PRIMARY SOURCE LIST

Page 4: First page of the *Massachusetts Spy*, a newspaper started by Isaiah Thomas in 1770. This page was from the July 7, 1774 issue, Volume IV, number 179.

Page 6: Portrait of Gilbert Motier, Marquis De La Fayette (Lafayette) by Joseph-Désiré Court (1797–1865), painted in 1834. The oil painting is housed at Réunion des musées nationaux.

Page 7: Engraving published in the *Life and Times of Washington, Volume 1,* 1857 by Alonzo Chappel (1828–1887).

Page 9: Engraving of the Battle of Brandywine by Johann Martin Will (1727–1806), created in 1777.

Page 10: Portrait of the King Louis XVI (1754–1793) by Joseph Siffred Duplessis (1725–1802). The oil painting was created in the 1770s. It is housed in the Musée Carnavalet, Paris, France.

Page 14: *Jean Baptiste Donatien de Vimeur, comte de Rochambeau* by Charles-Philippe Larivière (1798–1876). The oil painting was created in 1834.

Page 15: Oil painting, *Siege of Yorktown, 17th October 1781,* was created in 1836 by Louis Charles Auguste Couder (1790–1873).

Page 16: Oil portrait of François-Joseph-Paul, Count of Grasse (1722–1788), by Jean Baptiste Mauzaisse (1784–1844) in 1843. It is housed at the Chateaux de Versailles et de Trianon, Versailles, France.

Page 17: Illustration titled *Siege and Surrender at Yorktown* was created by H.C. Robertson in 1898.

WEBSITES

Due to the changing nature of Internet links, PowerKids Press has developed an online list of websites related to the subject of this book. This site is updated regularly. Please use this link to access the list: www.powerkidslinks.com/soah/marq